MENTAL NOTES

Complier/Designer/Illustrator:
Kate McDonnell

Editor:
Gideon Kibblewhite

First published 2015 by Tangent Books

Tangent Books
Unit 5.16 Paintworks
Bristol
BS4 3EH
0117 972 0645
www.tangentbooks.co.uk
Email: richard@tangentbooks.co.uk

ISBN 978-1-910089-12-5

MENTAL NOTES

Mental health quotes

Compiled and illustrated by Kate McDonnell
Edited by Gideon Kibblewhite

mind | Bath

for better mental health

Contents

Foreword

We live in a society where prejudice and unfairness still, sadly, surround mental health. So it is a brilliant thing when someone in the public eye stands up and says, "I am one of those 1 in 4 people who at any one time lives with a mental health problem."

When famous people speak out, it changes opinions, shapes attitudes and inspires people to seek help. And we know from those who call Mind's Infoline or visit our local Minds that, in sharing their stories, our celebrity ambassadors, including Mind's President, Stephen Fry, have helped others to feel it's okay to speak out.

In this by turns powerful and entertaining collection of quotes, famous and noted people from all walks of life give their thoughts on all kinds of mental health issues and on what it is like living with a mental health problem. Covering, chapter-by-chapter, a range of diverse subjects, from post-natal depression to mental health and art, this book highlights beautifully how fragile the human experience is and how that fragility can affect anyone.

For every well known person who speaks out about mental health there are many less famous people who are increasingly telling their own story and helping to change the way we think as a society. Equally, however, there are many more for whom the stigma of mental health remains too great. This book is about helping to counter that stigma and to think again.

Mental Notes was compiled and illustrated by Kate McDonnell for Bath Mind. All proceeds go to Bath Mind. You can find out more about Bath Mind, its work and how it can help, on page 140.

I hope you enjoy the book as much as I did.

Paul Farmer
CEO, Mind

Introduction

Mental Notes is a collection of quotations on the disorders of the mind from clinicians, writers, politicians and celebrities. Some are challenging, some insightful, some are funny, some just beautiful and sad. This fascinating read looks at psychotherapy, love, genius, art and much, much more.

An often startling collection of thoughts, **Mental Notes** shows how wonderful, but fragile we are and how common it is for people to suffer – even the very greatest people from history.

I started collecting quotes as a way to feel less alone in what I felt. As somebody who has bipolar disorder, I know that it is all too easy to become isolated. For many years I never had the courage to speak up, or even get help.

I hope you find these quotes as interesting, challenging and inspiring as I do.

Kate McDonnell

Disclaimer

Please be warned that some of the quotes in this book use language that some readers might not agree with, such as references to madness, lunacy, sanity and insanity, etc.

People who are vulnerable should be aware that some material could be triggering – especially the 'To Be Or Not To Be' chapter.

The views expressed are not necessarily those of Bath Mind.

ONE IN FOUR

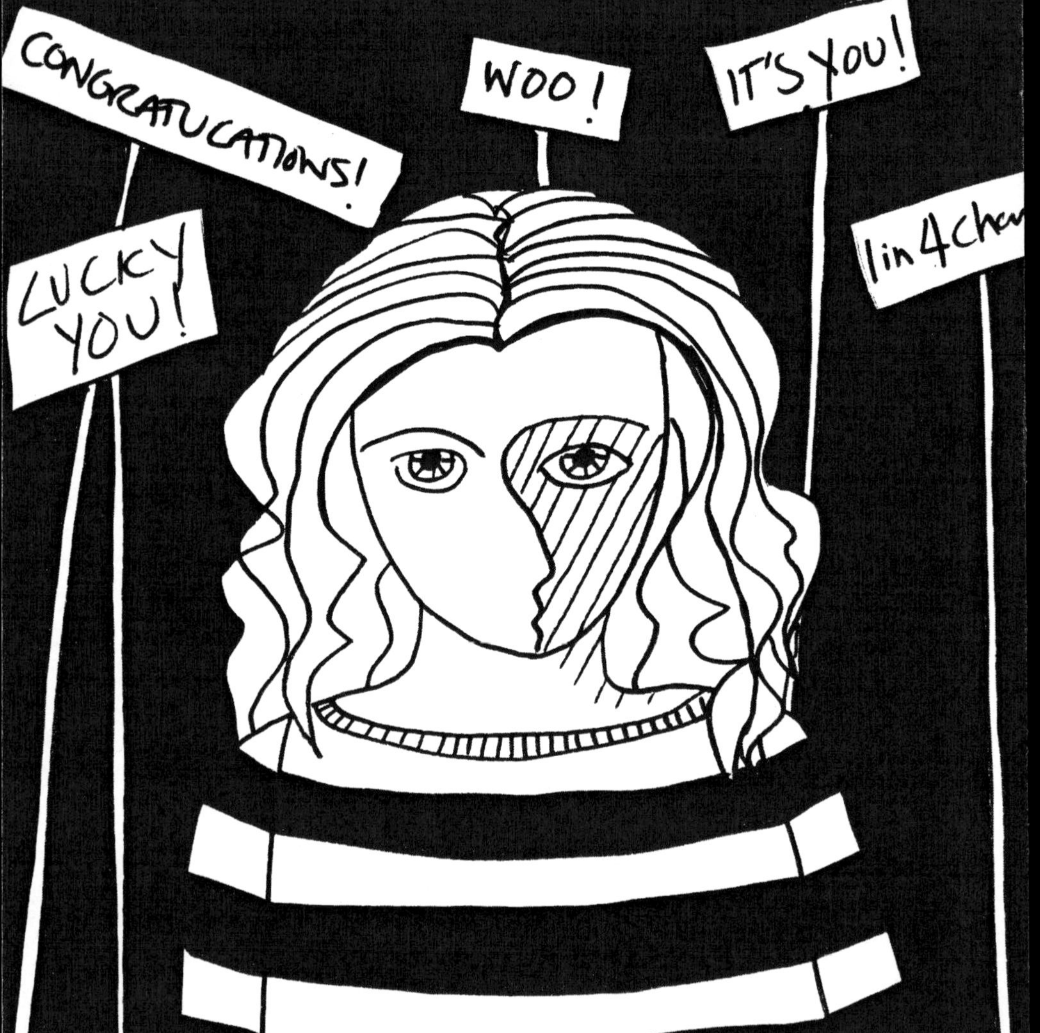

1 in 4 British adults experience at least one diagnosable mental health problem in any one year, and one in six experiences this at any given time.

— **Office for National Statistics**, *Psychiatric Morbidity report*, 2001

Mental health problems do not affect three or four out of every five persons but one out of one.

— **Dr. William Menninger**, psychiatrist (1899-1966), *New York Times*

"But I don't want to go among mad people," Alice remarked.

"Oh, you can't help that," said the Cat. "We're all mad here. I'm mad. You're mad."

"How do you know I'm mad?" said Alice.

"You must be," said the Cat. "or you wouldn't have come here."

— **Lewis Carroll**, author (1832-1898), *Alice in Wonderland*

There are materials enough in every man's mind to make a hell there.

– **Henry Ward Beecher,** social reformer (1813-1887),
Proverbs from Plymouth Pulpit

A child born today in the United Kingdom stands a ten times greater chance of being admitted to a mental hospital than to a university ... This can be taken as an indication that we are driving our children mad more effectively than we are genuinely educating them. Perhaps it is our way of educating them that is driving them mad.

– **R.D. Laing,** psychiatrist (1927-1989), *The Politics of Experience*

Maybe people are more like the earth than we know. Maybe they have fault lines that sooner or later are going to split open under pressure.

– **Rebecca Wells,** author, theatre director (1952-),
Divine Secrets of the Ya-Ya Sisterhood

I may be a lunatic, but then, wasn't my lunacy caused by a monster that lurks at the bottom of every human mind? Those who call me a madman and spurn me may become lunatics tomorrow. They harbour the same monster.

– **Akutagawa Ryunosuke**, author (1892-1927), *Doubts*

All are lunatics, but he who can analyse his delusions is called a philosopher.

– **Ambrose Bierce**, author (1842–1913), *Epigrams*

When we remember that we are all mad, the mysteries disappear and life stands explained.

– **Mark Twain**, author (1835-1910), *Notebook*

Crazy isn't being broken, or swallowing a dark secret. It's you or me, amplified.

– **Girl, Interrupted**, *film of the novel by Susanna Kaysen*

If man thinks about his physical or moral state he usually discovers that he is ill.
– **Johann Wolfgang von Goethe**, author (1749-1832), *Proverbs in Prose*

I think it's the rule rather than the exception; everyone is trying to cobble their lives together as best they can.
– **Darian Leader**, psychoanalyst (1965-), *interview, The Guardian*

Everybody's a mad scientist, and life is their lab. We're all trying to experiment to find a way to live, to solve problems, to fend off madness and chaos.
– **David Cronenberg**, film director (1943-), *Cronenberg on Cronenberg*

All living things contain a measure of madness that moves them in strange, sometimes inexplicable ways. This madness can be saving; it is part and parcel of the ability to adapt. Without it, no species would survive.
– **Yann Martel**, author (1963-), *Life of Pi*

We are all born mad. Some remain so.

— **Samuel Beckett**, novelist, playwright
(1906–1989), *Waiting for Godot*

I often say that we are all a little bit crazy and we don't know it, because people of the same craziness mix with their own kind. It is only when people differently crazy come together that they find out their own craziness.

— **Paramahansa Yogananda**, yogi, guru
(1893-1952), *Do Souls Reincarnate?*

The statistics on insanity are that one out of every four people is suffering from some form of mental illness. Think of your three best friends. If they're okay, then it's got to be you.

— **Rita Mae Brown**, author (1944-), *quoted by Susan Musgrave in Musgrave Landing: Musings on the Writing Life*

THE LAST TABOO

Mental illness is nothing to be ashamed of, but stigma and bias shame us all.

– **Bill Clinton**, US President (1946-), *presidential radio address*

Now, why is it that most of us can talk openly about the illnesses of our bodies, but when it comes to our brain and illnesses of the mind we clam up and because we clam up, people with emotional disorders feel ashamed, stigmatised, and don't seek the help that can make the difference.

– **Kirk Douglas**, actor (1916-), *My Stroke of Luck*

Those who do not feel pain seldom think that it is felt.

– **Samuel Johnson**, writer (1709-1784), *The Rambler*

Pain is real when you get other people to believe in it. If no one believes in it but you, your pain is madness or hysteria.

– **Naomi Wolf**, author (1962-), *The Beauty Myth*

Being considered or labelled mentally disordered – abnormal, crazy, mad, psychotic, sick, it matters not what variant is used – is the most profoundly discrediting classification that can be imposed on a person today. Mental illness casts the "patient" out of our social order just as surely as heresy cast the "witch" out of medieval society. That, indeed, is the very purpose of stigma terms.

– **Thomas Szasz**, psychiatrist (1920-2012),
The Manufacture of Madness

We cannot afford to postpone any longer a reversal in our approach to mental affliction. For too long the shabby treatment of the many millions of the mentally disabled in custodial institutions and any millions more now in communities needing help has been justified on grounds of inadequate funds, further studies and future promises.

– **John F. Kennedy**, US president (1917–1963),
message to Congress on Mental Health

Future generations will be amazed at how blind we were. They will also be amazed that we were so cruel.

– **Richard Layard**, economist (1934-), and **David Clark**, clinical psychologist (1954-), *Thrive*

[Madness] is the jail we could all end up in. And we know it. And watch our step. For a lifetime. We behave. A fantastic and entire system of social control, by the threat of example as effective over the general population as detention centres in dictatorships, the image of the madhouse floats through every mind for the course of its lifetime.

– **Kate Millett**, author and activist (1934-), *The Loony-Bin Trip*

For too long we have swept the problems of mental illness under the carpet and hoped that they would go away.

– **Richard J. Codey**, politician (1946-), *speech*

We all fear at some point that "our" world and "the" world are hopelessly estranged. Psychosis is the fulfilment of that fear.

– **Michael Greenberg**, author (1952-), *Hurry Down Sunshine*

When you look directly at an insane man all you see is a reflection of your own knowledge that he's insane, which is not to see him at all.

– **Robert M. Pirsig**, author and philosopher (1928-), *Zen and the Art of Motorcycle Maintenance*

You must always be puzzled by mental illness. The thing I would dread most, if I became mentally ill, would be your adopting a common sense attitude; that you could take it for granted that I was deluded.

– **Ludwig Wittgenstein**, philosopher (1889-1951), *quoted in Conversations with Wittgenstein by Maurice O'Connor Drury*

I am mentally ill. I can say that. I am not ashamed of that.

– **Carrie Fisher**, actor and writer (1956-), *interview, ABC News*

The extreme limit of wisdom, that's what the public calls madness.

– **Jean Cocteau**, novelist, filmmaker (1889-1963), *Cock and Harlequin*

Stress is nothing more than a socially acceptable form of mental illness.

– **Richard Carlson**, author, psychotherapist (1961-2006), *You Can be Happy No Matter What*

Before I realised I had depression, I used to say to people: 'You'll be fine, get over it,' but that's like telling a cancer victim: 'Get well.'

– **Kerry Katona**, musician (1980-), *interview, Mirror*

My twenties were a write-off. It [depression] is a cruel illness, because you can't see it and you can hide it so well.

– **Sarah Lancashire**, actress (1964-), *interview, Scotsman*

I'm scared of being alone in what I feel.

– **Doris Lessing**, author (1919-2013), *The Golden Notebook*

I was successful, rich and terribly unhappy.
I withdrew from the world and that
made me even more depressed. I can
understand why some people might
look at me and say, 'What's she got to be
depressed about?' I get that a lot in Britain,
where mental-health issues seem to be a
big taboo.

– **Natalie Imbruglia**, musician and actress (1975-),
interview, Daily Mail

I guess I never told anyone about the
pain I was going through because I didn't
understand it myself. It made no sense to
me that I felt so bad. How could I explain
something I couldn't understand?

– **Marcus Trescothick**, cricketer (1975-),
interview, Telegraph

Insanity is relative. It depends on who has
who locked in what cage.

– **Ray Bradbury**, author (1920-2012), *The Meadow*

Nothing defines the quality of life in a community more clearly than people who regard themselves, or whom the consensus chooses to regard, as mentally unwell.

– **Renata Adler**, author and journalist (1938-), *The Thursday Group*

This is a disorder that affects millions of people and I am one of them. If my revelation of having bipolar II has encouraged one person to seek help, then it is worth it. There is no need to suffer silently and there is no shame in seeking help.

– **Catherine Zeta-Jones**, actor (1969-),
statement to People magazine

If being sane is thinking there's something wrong with being different … I'd rather be completely fucking mental.

– **Angelina Jolie**, actor (1975-),
interview on Girl, Interrupted (film)

MAD WORLD

Insanity – a perfectly rational adjustment to an insane world.

– **R. D. Laing**, psychiatrist (1927-1989),
The Politics of Experience

We are in the process of creating what deserves to be called the idiot culture. Not an idiot sub-culture, which every society has bubbling beneath the surface and which can provide harmless fun; but the culture itself. For the first time, the weird and the stupid and the coarse are becoming our cultural norm, even our cultural ideal.

– **Carl Bernstein**, journalist (1944-),
New Republic

Schizophrenia is a special strategy that a person invents in order to live in an unlivable situation.

– **R. D. Laing**, psychiatrist (1927–1989),
The Divided Self

About a third of my cases are suffering from no clinically definable neurosis, but from the senselessness and emptiness of their lives. This can be defined as the general neurosis of our times.

– **Carl Jung**, psychiatrist (1875-1961),
Modern Man in Search of a Soul

We do not have to visit a madhouse to find disordered minds; our planet is the mental institution of the universe.

– **Johann Wolfgang von Goethe**,
poet and author (1749-1832), *attrib.*

The way it is now, the asylums can hold the sane people but if we tried to shut up the insane we would run out of building materials.

– **Mark Twain**, author (1835-1910),
Following The Equator

Our society is run by insane people for insane objectives … I think we're being run by maniacs for maniacal ends … and I think I'm liable to be put away as insane for expressing that. That's what's insane about it.

– **John Lennon**, musician (1940-1980), *interview, BBC2*

Maybe I'm needy, neurotic, paranoid. Under the circumstances, of course, if I weren't needy, neurotic, and paranoid, I'd obviously be psychotic.

– **Dean Koontz**, author (1945-), *Seize the Night*

I went into photography because it seemed like the perfect vehicle for commenting on the madness of today's existence.

– **Robert Mapplethorpe**, photographer (1946-1989), attrib.

Correct me if I'm wrong, but hasn't the fine line between sanity and madness gotten finer?

— **George Price**, geneticist (1922-1975), *attrib.*

And of course you are mad, if by a madman we mean a mind that questions and rejects every civilised norm.

— **Stephen Fry**, actor, writer, television presenter, President of Mind (1957-), *The Stars' Tennis Balls*

In a completely sane world, madness is the only freedom!

— **J. G. Ballard**, author (1930-2009), *interview, Re/Search*

Life is not a spectacle or a feast; it is a predicament.

— **George Santayana**, philosopher and poet (1863-1952), *Articles and Essays*

Men are so necessarily mad, that not to be mad would amount to another form of madness.

– Blaise Pascal, philosopher (1623-1662),
Thoughts

In a mad world, only the mad are sane.

– Akira Kurosawa, film director
(1910-1998), *Ran*

Who but the mad would choose to keep on living? In the end, aren't we all just a little crazy?

– Libba Bray, author (1964-),
Going Bovine

Perhaps God is not dead; perhaps God is himself mad.

– R.D. Laing, psychiatrist (1927-1989),
The Obvious

You know, there are many people in the country today who, through no fault of their own, are sane. Some of them were born sane. Some of them became sane later in their lives. It is up to people like you and me who are out of our tiny little minds to try and help these people overcome their sanity.

– **Graham Chapman**, comedian (1941-1989),
Monty Python's Flying Circus

I became insane, with long intervals of horrible sanity.

– **Edgar Allan Poe**, author (1809-1849), *letter*

Sanity is a cozy lie.

– **Susan Sontag**, author and activist (1933-2004),
Against Interpretation

Show me a sane man and I will cure him for you.

– **Carl Jung**, psychiatrist (1875-1961),
attributed to him by his assistant, Jolande Jacobi

When the world goes mad, one must accept madness as sanity; since sanity is, in the last analysis, nothing but the madness on which the whole world happens to agree.

– **George Bernard Shaw**, playwright (1856-1950),
an open letter to Gorki

What we call "normal" is a product of repression, denial, splitting, projection, introjection, and other forms of destructive actions on experience … It is radically estranged from the structure of being …

– **R. D. Laing**, psychiatrist (1927-1989),
The Politics of Experience

A man who is "of sound mind" is one who keeps the inner madman under lock and key.

– **Paul Valéry**, author, philosopher (1871-1945),
Mauvaises pensées et autres

Sanity is madness put to good use.

– **George Santayana**, philosopher
(1863 - 1952), *Little Essays*

There is a very fine line between 'hobby' and 'mental illness'.

— **Dave Barry**, author (1947-),
25 Things I Have Learned in 50 Years

Sanity remains defined simply by the ability to cope with insane conditions.

— **Ana Castillo**, poet, essayist (1953-),
Massacre of the Dreamers

Too much sanity may be madness. And maddest of all, to see life as it is and not as it should be.

— **Miguel de Cervantes Saavedra**, author
(1547–1616), *Don Quixote*

I always made a point of telling the doctors I was sane, and asking to be released, but the more I endeavoured to assure them of my sanity, the more they doubted it.

— **Nellie Bly (Elizabeth Jane Cochran)**, journalist
(1864-1922), *Ten Days in a Mad-House*

Mad, adj.: affected with a high degree of intellectual independence, not conforming to standards of thought, speech, and action derived by the conformants from the study of themselves; at odds with the majority; in short, unusual. It is noteworthy that persons are pronounced mad by officials destitute of evidence that they themselves are sane ...

– **Ambrose Bierce**, author (1842-1913),
The Devil's Dictionary

No man is sane who does not know how to be insane on proper occasions.

– **Henry Ward Beecher**, social reformer (1813-1887),
Proverbs from Plymouth Pulpit

But you learn to smother the living breathing soul, go deaf to it, and this violence to the self is what is commonly called sanity in the places where I have lived.

– **Philip Ó Ceallaigh**, writer (1968-),
Walking to the Danube

There is no insanity so devastating in man's life as utter sanity.

– **William Allen White**, journalist (1868-1944),
Forty Years on Main Street

The point is, you see … that there is no point driving yourself mad trying to stop yourself from going mad. You might just as well give in and save your sanity for later.

– **Douglas Adams**, author (1952-2001) ,
Life, the Universe and Everything

You wanted to get well … Asked your greatest wish in life, you would have replied at once – sanity … In the world outside, people longed desperately to be millionaires, movie actors, club presidents … But nowhere, nowhere save the madhouse, did mental health get its share of prayers.

– **Mary Jane Ward**, novelist (1905-1981),
The Snake Pit

THE FRAGILE MIND

Health is a state of complete physical, mental and social well-being, and not merely the absence of disease or infirmity.

– **World Health Organization**, 1948, *Constitution*

Diseases of the soul are more dangerous and more numerous than those of the body.

– **Cicero**, philosopher (106 BCE–43 BCE), *Tusculan Disputations*

Health of body and mind is a great blessing, if we can bear it.

– **John Henry Newman**, priest (1801–1890), *sermon*

An ill principle in the mind is worse than the matter of a disease in the body.

– **Benjamin Whichcote**, priest (1609–1683), *Moral and Religious Aphorisms*

The body's pain is so paper-thin and insignificant compared to that of the mind.

– **Peter Høeg**, author (1957-), *Smilla's Sense of Snow*

Nothing is at last sacred but the integrity of your own mind.

— **Ralph Waldo Emerson**, essayist, lecturer, poet
(1803-1882), *essay*

There is an elasticity in the human mind, capable of bearing much, but which will not show itself, until a certain weight of affliction be put upon it; its powers may be compared to those vehicles whose springs are so contrived that they get on smoothly enough when loaded, but jolt confoundedly when they have nothing to bear.

— **Charles Caleb Colton**, cleric, writer,
(1780-1832), *Lacon*

If there be a hell upon earth, it is to be found in a melancholy man's heart.

— **Robert Burton**, scholar (1577-1640),
The Anatomy of Melancholy

Insanity is often the logic of an accurate mind overtasked.

– **Oliver Wendell Holmes Sr.**, poet, physician, essayist (1809-1894), *The Autocrat of the Breakfast-Table*

The mind has no kitchen to do its dirty work in while the parlour remains clean.

– **Henry Ward Beecher**, social reformer (1813-1887), *Proverbs from Plymouth Pulpit*

What shall I compare it to, this fantastic thing I call my Mind? To a waste-paper basket, to a sieve choked with sediment, or to a barrel full of floating froth and refuse? No, what it is really most like is a spider's web, insecurely hung on leaves and twigs, quivering in every wind, and sprinkled with dewdrops and dead flies. And at its centre, pondering forever the Problem of Existence, sits motionless the spider-like and uncanny Soul.

– **Logan Pearsall Smith**, author (1865-1946), *Trivia*

The mind is its own place, and in itself
Can make a heaven of Hell,
a hell of Heaven.

– **John Milton**, poet (1608-1674), *Paradise Lost*

Some minds are so unclothed that they are indecent.

– **Austin O'Malley**, physician, humorist
(1858-1932), *Keystones of Thought*

The will ... is the driving force of the mind. If it's injured, the mind falls to pieces.

– **August Strindberg**, author, painter
(1849-1912), *The Father*

Babylon in all its desolation is a sight not so awful as that of the human mind in ruins.

– **Scrope Berdmore Davies**, clergyman (1708-1770), *letter*

When people will not weed their own minds, they are apt to be overrun with nettles.

– **Horace Walpole**, writer (1717-1797), *letter*

The mind goes on working no matter how we try to hold it back.

— **Frank Herbert**, author (1920-1986), *Dune*

What is madness but nobility of soul at odds with circumstance.

— **Theodore Roethke**, poet (1908-1963), *In a Dark Time*

A bodily disease, which we look upon as whole and entire within itself, may, after all, be but a symptom of some ailment in the spiritual part.

— **Nathaniel Hawthorne**, author (1804-1864), *The Scarlet Letter*

People think that if you're depressed, you're depressed about something, but I'm not, I just feel terrible. The real root of it all is that I suffer from an illness.

— **Robbie Williams**, musician (1974-), *quoted in Feel: Robbie Williams by Chris Heath*

When a man lacks mental balance in pneumonia he is said to be delirious. When he lacks mental balance without the pneumonia, he is pronounced insane by all smart doctors.

– **Martin H. Fischer**, physician, author (1879-1962),
quoted in Fischerisms by Howard Fabing and Ray Marr

Furiosi nulla voluntas est –
A madman has no free will.

– A legal phrase, *Latin for Lawyers by Sweet & Maxwell*

Whom Fortune wishes to destroy she first makes mad.

– **Publilius Syrus,** dramatist, writer
(*c.* 1st century BCE), *Moral Sayings*

We know the human brain is a device to keep the ears from grating one on another.

– **Peter de Vries,** writer (1910-1993),
Comfort me with Apples

"I must really improve my Mind," I tell myself, and once more begin to patch and repair that crazy structure. So I toil and toil on at the vain task of edification, though the wind tears off the tiles, the floors give way, the ceilings fall, strange birds build untidy nests in the rafters, and owls hoot and laugh in the tumbling chimneys.

– **Logan Pearsall Smith**, author (1865-1946), *Trivia*

I'd spend about an hour, my room darkening around me, wondering what the hell happened to make me so unsure of who I even was. Because who you are is supposed to be the easiest question in the world to answer, right? Only for me it hadn't been easy for a very long time.

– **Jennifer Brown**, author (1972-), *Hate List*

I have studiously tried to avoid ever using the word 'madness' to describe my condition. Now and again, the word slips out, but I hate it. 'Madness' is too glamorous a term to convey what happens to most people who are losing their minds. That word is too exciting, too literary, too interesting in its connotations, to convey the boredom, the slowness, the dreariness, the dampness of depression.

– **Elizabeth Wurtzel**, writer, journalist (1967-), *Prozac Nation*

A broken leg can be remembered and located: "It hurt right below my knee, it throbbed, I felt sick at my stomach." But mental pain is remembered the way dreams are remembered – in fragments, unbidden realizations, like looking into a well and seeing the dim reflection of your face in that instant before the water shatters.

– **Tracy Thompson**, journalist, author, editor (1955-), *The Beast: A Reckoning with Depression*

When I think of myself my mind cannot soar to higher things but is like a bird with broken wings.

– **Teresa of Ávila**, mystic, nun (1515-1582), *The Interior Castle*

People often write me and ask how I keep my wood floors so clean when I live with a child and a dog, and my answer is that I use a technique called Suffering From a Mental Illness.

– **Heather Armstrong**, blogger (1975-), *dooce.com*

Being a sex symbol is a heavy load to carry, especially when one is tired, hurt and bewildered.

– **Clara Bow**, actor (1926-1962), *attrib.*

I became depressed and I cut myself with scissors and stuff.

– **Dame Kelly Holmes**, athlete (1970-), *Desert Island Discs, Radio Four*

Returning to Earth was challenging for me. I was a celebrity on a pedestal, and I had to live up to that. Like actors and writers who are on and off again in terms of employment, I had a very unstructured life. So the alcoholism and depression, which I inherited, were ripe to flourish.

– **Buzz Aldrin**, astronaut (1930-), *Time magazine*

I used to think I was a drug addict, pure and simple - just someone who could not stop taking drugs willfully. And I was that. But it turns out that I am severely manic depressive.

– **Carrie Fisher**, actor and writer (1956-), *ABC News*

Some days I could get to the supermarket, but I could never go too far inside. I learned to cook with the ingredients they kept close to the door.

– **Paula Deen**, cook and TV personality (1947-), *interview, New York Times*

It affected everything–my family and friends. I was a pain in the arse to have around. I was miserable and self-absorbed.

– **Hugh Laurie**, actor (1959-),
interview, London Evening Standard

The lows were absolutely horrible. It was like falling into a manhole and not being able to lift the lid and climb out.

– **Linda Hamilton**, actress (1956-),
interview, AP Radio

It's a bit like walking down a long, dark corridor never knowing when the light will go on.

– **Neil Lennon**, footballer (1971-), *interview, Scotsman*

I have been cut in two.

– **Anne Sexton**, poet (1928-1974),
For the Year of the Insane

It's like a kettle. If it's a kettle, you turn the kettle off, you know what I mean? I wish I could put a hole in my head and let the steam come out. The pressure was just getting a little bit much for me.

– **Frank Bruno**, boxer (1961-), *interview, Scotsman*

I was horribly depressed, and I felt like I had failed as a band leader, a professional, as a person.

– **Ben Moody**, musician (1981-), *MTV*

You see the thing about depression is … that there is nothing wrong with you on the outside. I mean you know you don't have any lumps, or you don't have any scars. You are not in a wheelchair. So people go "Come on, come on!" Especially in England they say "Stiff upper lip; snap out of it." And you can't.

– **Ruby Wax**, comedian, TV presenter, Mind Ambassador (1953-), *video, time-to-change.org.uk*

I may have looked happy but inside I was hopelessly depressed.

— **Stephen Fry**, actor, writer, director, President of Mind (1957-),
The Secret Life Of The Manic Depressive

With depression, everyone runs in the opposite direction and no one wants to discuss it. It can be life-threatening – you lose your mind for a while and you can't get it back without assistance. It was a long slog back.

— **Trisha Goddard**, TV presenter (1957-), *Metro*

During the worst times, I shut the world out, refusing to get out of bed. Even the smallest tasks were overwhelming.

— **Shawn Colvin**, musician (1956-), *Beyond the Music campaign*

I really have a secret satisfaction in being considered rather mad.

— **William Heath Robinson**, illustrator (1872-1944),
personal epitaph

I hate to advocate drugs, alcohol, violence, or insanity to anyone, but they've always worked for me.

– **Hunter S. Thompson**, author and journalist (1937-2005), *quoted in Rolling Stone*

I didn't want anyone to think I was crazy, and I felt like I was going crazy.

– **Winona Ryder**, actor (1971-), *20 20 interview, ABC*

I didn't want to wake up. I was having a much better time asleep. And that's really sad. It was almost like a reverse nightmare, like when you wake up from a nightmare you're so relieved. I woke up into a nightmare.

– **Ned Vizzini**, writer (1981-2013), *It's Kind of a Funny Story*

You know what scares me? When you have to be nice to some paranoid schizophrenic, just because she lives in your body.

– **Judy Tenuta**, comedian (1956-), *comedy act*

Each time a breeze starts, I feel the air all the way through me.

                      – **Nina LaCour**, author (1982-), *Hold Still*

I don't think I would have really hurt myself but I was in a bad way … It was my lowest moment yet and I have had some low moments. In some ways it feels like it hasn't really happened, as if it happened to someone else.

                      – **Gail Porter**, TV presenter (1971-), *Mirror*

I couldn't cross the road, I didn't dare go into shops, I had to concentrate on breathing in and breathing out. It's panic attacks and you are on the brink of utter insanity.

                      – **Joanna Lumley**, actor (1946-), *Telegraph*

Things are always darkest just before they go pitch black.

                      – **Robert Culp**, actor, (1930-2010),
                      playing Kelly Robinson in TV show 'I spy'

So fit and healthy one day, mind, body and soul withering and dying the next. This to me is the most frightening of experiences.

– **Stan Collymore**, footballer (1971-), *via Twitter*

Living in Hollywood, you can get disconnected from everybody. You can feel like you are the only one. So you feel it, you hold it in and you don't let it go and you don't try to find help because you think, 'Oh man if I tell anybody, I'm going to seem like I'm weak. I won't get a movie deal. I won't get invited to …' whatever goes through your head.

– **Drew Carey**, actor and game show host (1958-), *interview, Access Hollywood, NBC*

I have a chronic sadness that recurs. The lowest point was in Australia in May. I was overwhelmingly sad, and I didn't know why, because I had all these things to be happy about.

– **Lady Gaga**, musician (1986-), *interview, Guardian*

I have got so low that I have asked to be hospitalised and for deep narcosis (sleep). I cannot stand being awake. The pain is too much ... Something has happened to me, this vital spark has stopped burning – I go to a dinner table now and I don't say a word, just sit there like a dodo. Normally I am the centre of attention, keeps the conversation going, – so that is depressing in itself. It's like another person taking over, very strange. The most important thing I say is 'good evening' and then I go quiet.

– **Spike Milligan**, comedian (1918-2002),
Depression and How to Survive It (with Anthony Clare)

Very depressed today. Unable to write a thing. Menacing gods. I feel outcast on a cold star, unable to feel anything but an awful helpless numbness.

– **Sylvia Plath**, poet and author (1932-63), *journal*

It was the worst day of my life - at the time - one during which, from waking with a hangover to rushing for a flight to Scotland, I felt a relentless march towards what, in my developing madness, I imagined was going to be my death.

– **Alastair Campbell**, journalist, political advisor, author, Mind Ambassador (1957-), *BBC News magazine*

There was a lot of stuff in the bank of emotional darkness, and, eventually, when I did make a withdrawal, I took it all out at once. I didn't just make a withdrawal as normal people do: every couple of weeks, they go to the hole in the wall and they take out their dose of pain and disappointment and rage and anger and betrayal and bitterness. I didn't make any withdrawal at all, until one day I went to the bank and emptied my entire vault.

– **Tony Slattery**, comedian (1959-), *Guardian*

I was sitting in my car, and I knew the gas was coming when I had an image of my mother finding me. She sacrificed so much for her children, and to end my life would be an incredibly selfish thing to do. It was all about a relationship. My sense of worth was so low.

– **Halle Berry**, actor (1966-), *interview, Parade magazine*

The parts of me that used to think I was different or smarter or whatever, almost made me die.

– **David Foster Wallace**, author (1962-2008), *quoted in Although Of Course You End Up Becoming Yourself by David Lipsky*

Should I kill myself, or have a cup of coffee?

– **Albert Camus**, author, journalist (1913-1960), *L'Étranger*

While it is true that the suicide braves death, he does it not for some noble object but to escape some ill.

– **Aristotle**, philosopher (384-322 BCE), *Nicomachean Ethics*

What difference is there between a smoker and a suicide, except that the one takes longer to kill himself than the other.

– **Jacob Balde**, preacher (*c.* 1658), *attrib.*

Suicide is the worst form of murder, because it leaves no opportunity for repentance.

– **John Churton Collins**, literary critic (1848-1908), *quoted by L. C. Collins in Life and Memoirs of John Churton Collins*

There are many who dare not kill themselves for fear of what the neighbours will say.

– **Cyril Connolly**, journalist, writer (1903-1974), *The Unquiet Grave*

Each advancing age period of life shows a steady and consistent rise in suicide frequency.

– **Louis I. Dublin**, epidemiologist (*c.* 1890-1970), *attrib.*

Suicide is not a remedy.

– **James A. Garfield**, US president (1831-1881), *presidential inaugural address*

I take it that no man is educated who has never dallied with the thought of suicide.

– **William James,** psychologist (1842-1910), *attrib.*

Statistical evidence shows that the greater the intellectual freedom, and the higher the general average of intelligence in a community, the greater is also the number of suicides.

– **Svend Ranulf,** sociologist (1894-1953),
The Jealousy of the Gods and Criminal Law at Athens

I don't like standing near the edge of a platform when an express train is passing through. I like to stand right back and if possible get a pillar between me and the train. I don't like to stand by the side of a ship and look down into the water. A second's action would end everything. A few drops of desperation.

– **Winston Churchill,** British prime minister (1874-1965),
Churchill Taken From the Diaries of Lord Moran

Suicide. A sideways word, a word that people whisper and mutter and cough: a word that must be squeezed out behind cupped palms or murmured behind closed doors. It was only in dreams that I heard the word shouted, screamed.

– **Lauren Oliver**, author (1982-), *Delirium*

I had developed manic depression [bipolar disorder] … and the main symptom is the constant voice in the head telling you to kill yourself.

– **Sinéad O'Connor**, musician (1966-), *Independent*

The thought of suicide is a great consolation: by means of it one gets through many a dark night.

– **Friedrich Nietzsche**, philosopher (1844-1900), *Beyond Good and Evil*

We cannot tear out a single page of our life, but we can throw the whole book in the fire.

– **George Sand**, author (1804-76), *Mauprat*

I feel certain that I'm going mad again, I feel we can't go through another of those terrible times. And I shan't recover this time. I begin to hear voices.

– **Virginia Woolf**, author (1882-1941), *suicide letter*

"Did you really want to die?"
"No one commits suicide because they want to die."
"Then why do they do it?"
"Because they want to stop the pain."

– **Tiffanie DeBartolo**, author, director (1970-),
How to Kill a Rock Star

One night some short weeks ago, for the first time in her not always happy life, Marilyn Monroe's soul sat down alone to a quiet supper from which it did not rise. If they tell you that she died of sleeping pills you must know that she died of a wasting grief, of a slow bleeding at the soul.

– **Clifford Odets**, playwright, director (1906-63),
Show magazine

Melancholy suicide. This is connected with a general state of extreme depression and exaggerated sadness, causing the patient no longer to realise sanely the bonds which connect him with people and things about him.

– **Émile Durkheim**, sociologist (1858-1917),
Suicide: A Study in Sociology

Killing oneself is, anyway, a misnomer. We don't kill ourselves. We are simply defeated by the long, hard struggle to stay alive. When somebody dies after a long illness, people are apt to say, with a note of approval, "He fought so hard." And they are inclined to think, about a suicide, that no fight was involved, that somebody simply gave up. This is quite wrong.

Sally Brampton, author (1955-),
Shoot the Damn Dog: A Memoir of Depression

When people kill themselves, they think they're ending the pain, but all they're doing is passing it on to those they leave behind.

– **Jeannette Walls**, author (1960-), *Half Broke Horses*

After losing my job, I felt the only options available to me were razors, cyanide, or a shot to the face, until Renaldo, being the good friend that he is, reminded me how to tie a noose.

Jarod Kintz, author (1982-), *The Days of Yay are Here!*
Wake Me Up When They're Over.

No man ever threw away life while it was worth keeping.

David Hume, philosopher (1711-1776), *Of Suicide*

Suicide only really frightens those who are never tempted by it and never will be, for its darkness only welcomes those who are predestined to it.

– **Georges Bernanos**, author (1888-1948), *Mouchette*

I mentally bless and exonerate anyone who has kicked a chair out from beneath her or swallowed opium in large chunks. My mind has met their environment, here in the void. I understand perfectly.

– **Suzanne Finnamore**, journalist, author (1960-),
Split: A Memoir of Divorce

Anyway, during that period with the Police, the most successful time of my life, I was suicidal. My first marriage and my relationship with the other members of the band was collapsing. I just felt adrift. I was manic-depressive and I just wasn't chemically balanced enough to enjoy it. I was out to lunch.

– **Sting**, musician (1951-), *Live! magazine*

The only difference between a suicide and a martyrdom really is the amount of press coverage.

– **Chuck Palahniuk**, novelist, journalist (1962 -), *Survivor*

It is not seen as insane when a fighter, under an attack that will inevitable lead to his death, chooses to take his own life first. In fact, this act has been encouraged for centuries, and is accepted even now as an honourable reason to do the deed. How is it any different when you are under attack by your own mind?

– **Emilie Autumn**, musician, poet (1979-),
The Asylum for Wayward Victorian Girls

Nothing in my life has ever made me want to commit suicide more than people's reaction to my trying to commit suicide.

– **Emilie Autumn**, musician, poet (1979-),
The Asylum for Wayward Victorian Girls

I know, too, that death is the only god who comes when you call.

– **Roger Zelazny**, writer (1937-1995), *Frost and Fire*

Keep passing the open windows.

– **John Irving**, novelist, screenwriter (1942-),
The Hotel New Hampshire

The awareness of the damage done by severe mental illness – to the individual himself and to others – and fears that it may return again play a decisive role in many suicides.

– **Kay Redfield Jamison**, clinical psychologist (1946-), Night Falls Fast: Understanding Suicide

When you're young and healthy you can plan on Monday to commit suicide, and by Wednesday you're laughing again.

– **Marilyn Monroe**, actor (1926-1962), *My Story*

The red washing
down the bathtub
can't change the colour
of the sea at all.

– **Derrick C. Brown**, poet (1973-), *Instead of Killing Yourself*

EVERYDAY CRAZY

The average, healthy, well-adjusted adult gets up at seven-thirty in the morning feeling just plain terrible.

– **Jean Kerr,** dramatist (1923-2003), *Please Don't Eat the Daisies*

No one is moved to act, or resolves to speak a single word, who does not hope by means of this action or word to release anxiety from his spirit.

– **Ali Ibn Hazm,** theologian (994-1064),
Epistle on the to Apply to Souls Sect

Solitude is a torment which is not threatened in hell itself.

– **John Donne,** poet (1572-1631), *Awakenings*

Reality is the leading cause of stress amongst those in touch with it.

– **Jane Wagner,** playwright, actress (1935-),
The Search for Signs of Intelligent Life in the Universe

Drunkenness is nothing but
voluntary madness.

– **Seneca**, philosopher (4 BCE-65 CE),
Epistulae ad Lucilium

Every form of addiction is bad, no matter
whether the narcotic be alcohol or
morphine or idealism.

– **Carl Jung**, psychiatrist (1875-1961),
Memories, Dreams, Reflections

Drunkenness, the ruin of reason, the
destruction of strength, premature old
age, momentary death.

– **Basil of Caesarea**, bishop (*c.* 300-379CE), *Homilies*

What is childhood but a series of
happy delusions?

– **Sydney Smith**, clergyman (1771-1845), *quoted in*
A Memoir of the Rev. Sydney Smith

Everybody's youth is a dream, a form of chemical madness.

– **F. Scott Fitzgerald**, author (1896-1940),
The Diamond as Big as the Ritz

Innocence is a kind of insanity.

– **Graham Greene**, author (1904-91), *The Quiet American*

The misery of a child is interesting to a mother, the misery of a young man is interesting to a young woman, the misery of an old man is interesting to nobody.

– **Victor Hugo**, writer (1802-85), Les Misérables

What makes old age hard to bear is not the failing of one's faculties, mental and physical but the burden of one's memories.

– **W. Somerset Maugham**, writer, doctor
(1874-1965), *Points of View*

It's not catastrophes, murders, deaths,
diseases, that age and kill us;
it's the way people look and laugh,
and run up the steps of omnibuses.

– **Virginia Woolf**, author (1882-1941), *Jacob's Room*

The monsters of the mind are far worse
than those that actually exist. Fear, doubt,
and hate have hamstrung more people
than beasts ever have.

– **Christopher Paolini**, author (1983-), *Brisingr*

Optimism is the madness of insisting that all
is well when we are miserable.

– **Voltaire**, philosopher (1694-1778), *Candide*

The definition of insanity is doing the
same thing over and over and expecting a
different result.

– **Narcotics Anonymous** *Basic Text, 1981 ed.*

I am a clean-hands freak … there is no way, after shaking someone's hand, that I would eat bread … if any of you folks reading this book really like me, please approach me a any time, in a restaurant or elsewhere, and don't stick out your hand but simply bow. I will bow back and greatly appreciate the thought.

– **Donald Trump**, business magnate, TV personality (1946-), *The Art of the Comeback*

I definitely have not been happy. Especially when I had that second surgery (on my foot), I was definitely depressed. I cried all the time. I was miserable to be around.

– **Serena Williams**, athlete (1981-), *USA Today*

Anger is a short madness.

– **Horace**, poet (65 BCE-8 BCE), *Epistles*

What else is there to do in college except drink beer or slit one's wrists?

– Bret Easton Ellis, author (1964-), *The Rules of Attraction*

Madness wrenches us from the common language of life.

– Michael Greenberg, author (1952-), *Hurry Down Sunshine*

All extremes of feeling are allied with madness.

– Virginia Woolf, author (1882-1941), *Orlando*

There is a kind of euphoria of grief, a degree of madness.

– Nigella Lawson, food writer, broadcaster (1960-), *interview, Guardian*

Insanity doesn't run in my family. It gallops.

– Cary Grant, actor (1904-86), *Arsenic and Old Lace*

I believe that always, or almost always, in all childhoods and in all the lives that follow them, the mother represents madness. Our mothers always remain the strangest, craziest people we've ever met.

– **Marguerite Duras**, writer, film director
(1914-1996), *Practicalities*

My father had a profound influence on me; he was a lunatic.

– **Spike Milligan**, comedian (1918-2002), *quoted by Norma Farnes in Memories of Milligan*

To put meaning in one's life may
end in madness,
But life without meaning is the torture
Of restlessness and vague desire -
It is a boat longing for the sea
and yet afraid.

– **Edgar Lee Masters**, poet (1868-1950), *George Gray*

Love is like the measles, we all have to go through it.

— **Jerome K. Jerome**, humorist (1859-1927),
Idle Thoughts of an Idle Fellow

The functional form of impotence fills the coffers of the quacks, and swells the list of suicides.

— **Rutherford Morrison**, surgeon
(1853-1939), *The Practitioner*

Sex is not an antidote for loneliness, feelings of inadequacy, fear of aging, hostility, or an inability to form warm friendships.

— **Isabel P. Robinault,** sexologist,
Sex, Society and the Disabled

If this be not love, it is madness, and then it is pardonable.

— **William Congreve**, playwright, poet
(1670-1729), *The Old Batchelor*

If an individual is able to love productively, he loves himself too; if he can love only others, he cannot love at all.

– **Erich Fromm**, psychoanalyst, sociologist
(1900-1980), *The Art of Loving*

There is always some madness in love. But there is also always some reason in madness.

– **Friedrich Nietzsche**, philosopher (1844-1900),
Thus Spoke Zarathustra

You call it madness, but I call it love.

– *song by* **Gladys Dubois, Con Conrad,
Russ Columbo, Paul Gregory,** *1931*

Well, love is insanity. The ancient Greeks knew that. It is the taking over of a rational and lucid mind by delusion and self-destruction. You lose yourself, you have no power over yourself, you can't even think straight.

– **Marilyn French**, author (1929-2009),
The Women's Room

Love lyrics have contributed to the general aura of bad mental health in America.

— **Frank Zappa**, musician (1940-1993),
interview, The Curmodgeon by Jon Winokur

Romantic love is mental illness. But it's a pleasurable one. It's a drug. It distorts reality, and that's the point of it. It would be impossible to fall in love with someone that you really saw.

— **Fran Lebowitz**, author (1950-), *quoted in*
A Curmudgeon's Garden of Love by Jon Winokur

Jealousy lives upon doubts. It becomes madness or ceases entirely as soon as we pass from doubt to certainty.

— **François duc de La Rochefoucauld**, author (1613-80),
Moral Reflections, Sentences and Maxims

Most, if not all, problems brought to therapists are issues of love. It makes sense that the cure is also love.

— **Thomas Moore**, author, psychotherapist
(1940-), *Care of the Soul*

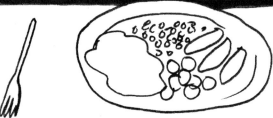

"My arms were so skinny that I couldn't pull myself out of a pool. I wasn't bulimic, but I could understand what people go through with that … I'd look in the mirror and still see a 180-lb. guy, even though I was 138 pounds.

– **Dennis Quaid**, actor (1954-),
interview, Best Life magazine

"I would eat 300 calories a day - a lot of Jell-O and no-sugar everything, of course. I was doing Pilates, weight-training, circuit training; over lunch I would run on a treadmill in my dressing room with a fan on my face so I wouldn't sweat my makeup off.

– **Portia de Rossi**, actor (1973-),
People magazine

"I've still got the scars on my knuckles from where I put my fingers down my throat.

– **Thandie Newton**, actor (1972-),
interview, Easy Living magazine

I started under-eating, over-exercising, pushing myself too hard and brutalizing my immune system. I guess I just didn't find time to eat.

– **Calista Flockhart**, actor (1964-), *Mirror*

I can honestly tell you from personal experience, that worrying about an eating disorder really can get you down. There's nothing to be ashamed about. You'll be amazed at the difference it'll make to your whole life if you tell someone you trust. There are lots of people who want to help and you really can't fight this one on your own. It might be a hard decision to make, to tell people and to seek help but, trust me it's nowhere as hard as trying to deal with it on your own.

– **Geri Halliwell**, musician (1972-), *OK! magazine*

I had bulimia for a number of years. And that's like a secret disease. You inflict it upon yourself because your self esteem is at a low ebb, and you don't think you're worthy or valuable. You fill your stomach up four or five times a day, some do it more, and it gives you a feeling of comfort. It's like having a pair of arms around you, but it's temporary. Then you're disgusted at the bloatedness of your stomach, and then you bring it all up again and it's a repetitive pattern which is very destructive to yourself.

– **Diana, Princess of Wales**, (1961-1997), *interview, Panorama, BBC*

I still have bulimia, Ozzy knows and the kids - my God, how could they not. It's the thing that causes most arguments. "We'll be at the dinner table and I'll go off and they'll say, 'Oh, here we go again.' They hate it.

– **Sharon Osbourne**, TV personality (1952-), *Daily Mail*

The things I wanted in life - I wanted to get married, I wanted to act, I wanted to have a career, to have kids - all those things, anorexia stood in the way of.

> – **Tracey Gold**, actor (1969-), *interview, ABC News*

I was anorexic for many, many years—even before people knew what it was. They didn't even have a name for it back then.

> – **Sandra Dee**, actor (1942-2005), *interview, National Inquirer*

I was very obsessed. I mean, I could tell you the fat content and the calorie content in absolutely anything.

> – **Victoria Beckham**, musician, fashion designer (1974-), *interview, ABC*

Anorexia is such a self-consuming, selfish disease. It's all about you. Becoming a mother, all of a sudden it wasn't about me anymore.

> – **Tracey Gold**, actor (1969-), *interview, CNN*

I had a brief flirtation with anorexia and when I was recovering from that, I put on a lot of weight, which was very difficult for me. In a way, I was trying to get rid of my breasts. Everyone my age wanted them, so it was like, whoo-ooo. Then I started hating them. And for all of my movies, I was supposed to be younger, so I'd have to strap them down.

– **Christina Ricci**, actor (1980-),
interview, Mademoiselle magazine

I did it all: anorexia, bulimia, binging, over-exercise. But no matter how much weight I lost I could never look "skinny". It's not my body type! So I always felt disgusting and like a failure. I hated myself and my body, but always tried to hide how I felt behind a smile. It was my secret shame.

– **Barbara Niven**, actor (1953-), *official website*

I had been on this insane diet for almost 17 years to maintain the weight that was demanded of me when I was modelling. My diet was really starvation. I am not naturally that thin, so I had to go through everything from using drugs to diet pills to laxatives to fasting.

– **Carré Otis**, model, actress (1968-), *USA Today*

I am forever engaged in a silent battle in my head over whether or not to lift the fork to my mouth, and when I talk myself into doing so, I taste only shame. I have an eating disorder.

– **Jena Morrow**, author, activist, *Hollow: An Unpolished Tale*

I always felt that anorexia was the form of breakdown most readily available to adolescent girls.

– **Kate Beckinsale**, actor (1973-), *Interview magazine*

Overeating is the addiction of choice of carers, and that's why it's come to be regarded as the lowest-ranking of all the addictions. It's a way of fucking yourself up while still remaining fully functional, because you have to. Fat people aren't indulging in the "luxury" of their addiction making them useless, chaotic, or a burden. Instead, they are slowly self-destructing in a way that doesn't inconvenience anyone … All the quietly eating mums. All the KitKats in office drawers. All the unhappy moments, late at night, caught only in the fridge light.

– **Caitlin Moran**, broadcaster, journalist (1975-), *How to Be a Woman*

Obesity is a mental state, a disease brought on by boredom and disappointment.

– **Cyril Connolly**, journalist, writer (1903-1974), *The Unquiet Grave*

Gluttony is an emotional escape, a sign something is eating us.

– **Peter de Vries**, writer (1910-1993), *Comfort Me with Apples*

BABY BLUES

The hardest part for me was acknowledging the problem … I thought postpartum depression meant you were sobbing every single day and incapable of looking after a child. But there are different shades of it and depths of it, which is why I think it's so important for women to talk about. It was a trying time. I felt like a failure.

— **Gwyneth Paltrow**, actor (1972-),
interview, Good Housekeeping magazine

I just felt as though I would never be happy again, and as if I had fallen into a big black hole.

— **Brooke Shields**, actress (1965-), *Down Came the Rain*

We think and we feel that we should just be able to handle it on our own.

— **Brooke Shields**, actress (1965-), *speech, Hope for Depression Research Foundation awards*

The doctor had warned me to go easy, but I thought his advice was for somebody else … Five minutes later, I was sitting on the kitchen floor, heaving with sobs and all I could think was, "This can't be happening to me." This couldn't be me, collapsing in hysteria, not even recognizing my own wails. This was not me, shaken to the core, sliding into a despair of the deepest kind. Whoever this was, she had no control of her emotions. Whoever this was, I wanted nothing to do with her. I wanted her away from my house, my children, and my baby.

– **Marie Osmond**, musician, actor (1959-), *Behind the Smile*

One out of every seven new mothers has post-natal depression - but, according to the Fatherhood Institute, one out of every 10 fathers are depressed both before and after their baby is born.

– **BBC News**, *2011*

You'd wake up in the morning feeling you didn't want to get out of bed. You felt misunderstood. I had never had a depression in my life.

– **Diana, Princess of Wales**, (1961-1997), *interview, Panarama, BBC*

I went through a really hard time … when (Coco) turned 6 months. I couldn't sleep. My heart was racing. And I got really depressed. I went to the doctor and found out my hormones had been pummelled.

– **Courteney Cox**, actor (1964-), *interview, USA Today*

It was more painful and took longer to lift. I felt suicidal. I couldn't stop crying - at playgroup, in the car, at home. I remember thinking 'Wouldn't it be great if the car crashed and I died?'

– **Melinda Messenger**, model, TV presenter (1971-), *Mirror*

MONEY MATTERS

I read somewhere that 77 per cent of all the mentally ill live in poverty. Actually, I'm more intrigued by the 23 per cent who are apparently doing quite well for themselves.

– **Emo Philips**, comedian (1956-), *Montreal Comedy Festival*

The strongest predictor of unhappiness is anyone who has had a mental illness in the last 10 years. It is an even stronger predictor of unhappiness than poverty – which also ranks highly.

– **Polly Toynbee**, journalist (1946-), *Guardian*

There is no better therapy than a job and a paycheck.

– **Dr. William C. Menninger**, (1899-1966), *quoted in Mental Hygiene*

Those with the money are eccentric. Those without, insane.

– **Bruce Robinson**, actor, screenwriter, director (1946-), *Withnail and I*

The greatest disease in the West today is not TB or leprosy; it is being unwanted, unloved, and uncared for. We can cure physical diseases with medicine, but the only cure for loneliness, despair, and hopelessness is love. There are many in the world who are dying for a piece of bread but there are many more dying for a little love.

– **Mother Teresa**, nun (1910-1997), *A Simple Path*

People with low levels of social support and from poorer backgrounds were more likely to develop suicidal thoughts and, once they had developed them, were less likely to recover.

– **The Office for National Statistics**, *Better or Worse: A Longitudinal Study of the Mental Health of Adults in Great Britain*, 2003

I had noticed that both in the very poor and very rich extremes of society the mad were often allowed to mingle freely.

– **Charles Bukowski**, poet, author (1920-94), *Ham on Rye*

Last time I talked to her she didn't sound like herself. She's depressed. It's awful what happens when people run out of money. They start thinking they're no good.

– **Barbara Kingsolver**, author (1955-), *Pigs in Heaven*

But money spent while manic doesn't fit into the Internal Revenue Service concept of medical expense or business loss. So after mania, when most depressed, you're given excellent reason to be even more so.

– **Kay Redfield Jamison**, clinical psychologist (1946-), *An Unquiet Mind*

Howard Hughes was able to afford the luxury of madness, like a man who not only thinks he is Napoleon but hires an army to prove it.

– **Ted Morgan**, journalist, author (1932-), *New York Times Book Review*

If a patient is poor he is committed to a public hospital as 'psychotic'; if he can afford the luxury of a private sanitarium, he is put there with the diagnosis of 'neuroasthenia'; if he is wealthy enough to be isolated in his own home under constant watch of nurses and physicians he is simply an indisposed 'eccentric'.

– **Pierre Marie Janet**, psychologist (1859-1947),
Strength and Psychological Debility

The population of the United States is beyond that of other countries, an anxious one. All classes are either striving after wealth, or endeavouring to keep up appearances.

– **Benjamin McCready,** physician (1813-1892),
Transactions of the Medical Society of the State of New York

The distance between insanity and genius is measured only by success.

– **Bruce Feirstein**, screenwriter, humorist (1956-),
film, Tomorrow Never Dies

I saw the best minds of my generation destroyed by madness, starving hysterical naked.

– **Allen Ginsberg**, poet (1926-1997), *Howl*

The bravest sight in the world is to see a great man struggling against adversity.

– **Seneca**, philosopher (4 BCE–65 CE), *De Providentia*

There is in every madman a misunderstood genius whose idea, shining in his head, frightened people, and for whom delirium was the only solution to the strangulation that life had prepared for him.

– **Antonin Artaud**, actor, producer (1896-1948),
Van Gogh, the Man Suicided by Society

The thoughts written on the walls of madhouses by their inmates might be worth publicising.

– **Georg Christoph Lichtenberg**, scientist (1742-1799), *The Waste Books*

Everything great in the world is done by neurotics; they alone founded our religions and created our masterpieces.

– **Marcel Proust**, author (1871-1922), *À la Recherche du Temps Perdu*

There's a fine line between genius and insanity. I have erased this line.

– **Oscar Levant**, actor (1906-1972), *The Jack Parr Tonight Show*

There was never a genius without a tincture of madness.

– **Aristotle**, philosopher (384-322 BCE),
quoted by Seneca in Problemata

I quite agree with Dr. Nordau's assertion that all men of genius are insane, but Dr. Nordau forgets that all sane people are idiots.

– **Oscar Wilde**, writer, poet (1854-1900),
quoted by Chris Healy in Confessions of a Journalist

THE JOY OF MADNESS

You're only given a little spark of madness. You mustn't lose it.

— **Robin Williams**, actor, comedian (1951-2014), *Funny Business*

There is a pleasure, sure, in being mad, which none but madmen know!

— **John Dryden**, poet, playwright (1631-1700), *The Spanish Friar*

The place where optimism most flourishes is the lunatic asylum.

— **Havelock Ellis**, psychologist (1859-1939), *The Dance of Life*

There is no evidence that we've been placed on this planet to be especially happy or especially normal. And in fact our unhappiness and our strangeness, our anxieties and compulsions, those least fashionable aspects of our personalities, are quite often what lead us to do rather interesting things.

— **Jon Ronson**, journalist (1967-),
The Psychopath Test

A person needs a little madness, or else they
never dare cut the rope and be free.

– **Nikos Kazantzakis**, writer, philosopher
(1883-1957), *Zorba the Greek*

**Men have called me mad; but the question
is not yet settled, whether madness be or
be not the loftier intelligence.**

– **Edgar Allan Poe**, author (1809-1849), *Eleonora*

Oh! thou who art greatly mad, deign to spare
me who am less mad.

– **Horace**, poet (65-8 BCE), *Satires*

For me, the adventures of the mind, each
inflection of thought, each movement,
nuance, growth, discovery, is a source
of exhilaration.

– **Anais Nin**, author (1903-1977), *diary*

So long as man is protected by madness - he functions - and flourishes.

– **Emile M. Cioran**, philosopher (1911-1995),
Précis de décomposition

I think sometimes depression is a trigger for us to get out of the old habits we learned as we grew up ... to decide for ourselves how we will react to what is around us.

– **Brian May**, musician (1947-),
Desert Island Discs, Radio Four

See, the human mind is kind of like... a piñata. When it breaks open, there's a lot of surprises inside. Once you get the piñata perspective, you see that losing your mind can be a peak experience.

– **Jane Wagner**, author, director (1935-),
The Search for Signs of Intelligent Life in the Universe

> Those who don't know how to weep with their whole heart don't know how to laugh either.

– **Golda Meir**, Israeli prime minister (1898-1978), *interview, Ms. magazine*

> For me, insanity is supersanity. The normal is psychotic – a collective psychosis. Normal means lack of imagination, lack of creativity.

– **Jean Dubuffet**, artist (1901-1985), *New Yorker*

> We derive our vitality from our store of madness.

– **Emile M. Cioran**, philosopher, essayist (1911-1995), *La Tentation d'Exister*

> Madness is tonic and invigorating. It makes the sane more sane. The only ones who are unable to profit by it are the insane.

– **Henry Miller**, author, painter (1891-1980), *The Cosmological Eye*

> I sometimes wonder how all those who do not write, compose, or paint can manage to escape the madness, the melancholia, the panic-fear which is inherent in the human situation.

– **Graham Greene**, author (1904-1991), *Ways of Escape*

> I never found out until I went into treatment that I was bipolar. Looking back it makes sense … There were times when I was so manic, I was writing seven songs in one night and I'd be up until 5:30 in the morning.

– **Demi Lovato**, musician (1992-), *Good Morning America, ABC*

> To write poetry and to commit suicide, apparently so contradictory, had really been the same, attempts at escape.

– **John Fowles**, author (1926-2005), *The Magus*

> A book is a suicide postponed.

– **Emil Cioran**, philosopher (1911-1995), *De l'Inconvenient d'Etre Ne*

I make films because if I don't make them then I don't have anything to distract me. My whole life I am constantly fighting all kinds of depression and terror and anxiety and I find that, like a mental patient in an institution, that if they keep the patient busy finger painting then they are more relaxed.

– **Woody Allen**, screenwriter, director, actor (1935-),
press launch, Match Point

My fear of life is necessary to me, as is my illness. Without anxiety and illness, I am a ship without a rudder. My art is grounded in reflections over being different from others. My sufferings are part of my self and my art. They are indistinguishable from me, and their destruction would destroy my art. I want to keep those sufferings.

– **Edvard Munch**, artist (1863–1944), *journal*

The only thing I could do was write.
I used to crawl from the bedroom to the
computer and just sit and write, and then
I was alright, because I was not present.
Sense and Sensibility really saved me from
going under, I think, in a very nasty way.

– **Emma Thompson**, actor, writer (1959-),
Desert Island Discs, Radio 4

The courage of the poet is to keep ajar the
door that leads into madness.

– **Christopher Morley**, author, poet, journalist
(1890-1957), *Inward Ho!*

A young man is afraid of his demon and
puts his hand over the demon's mouth
sometimes and speaks for him. And the
things the young man says are very
rarely poetry.

– **D.H. Lawrence**, author (1885-1930),
preface to Collected Poems

Did the hospital specialise in poets and singers, or was it that poets and singers specialised in madness?

– **Susanna Kaysen**, author (1948-), *Girl, Interrupted*

Science is for those who learn; poetry, for those that know.

– **Joseph Roux**, priest (1834-1886), *Meditations of a Parish Priest*

When you live in the shadow of insanity, the appearance of another mind that thinks and talks as yours does is something close to a blessed event.

– **Robert M. Pirsig**, author, philosopher (1928-), *Zen and the Art of Motorcycle Maintenance*

What garlic is to salad, insanity is to art.

– **Augustus Saint-Gaudens**, artist, (1848-1907), *The Reminiscences of Augustus Saint-Gaudens*

We work in the dark - we do what we can - we give what we have. Our doubt is our passion and our passion is our task. The rest is the madness of art.

— **Henry James**, author (1843-1916), *The Middle Years*

If poets often commit suicide, it is not because their poems are bad but because they are good. Whoever heard of a bad poet committing suicide? The reader is only a little better off. The exhilaration of a good poem lasts twenty minutes, an hour at most. Unlike the scientist, the artist has reentry problems that are frequent and catastrophic.

— **Walker Percy**, author (1916-1990), *Lost in the Cosmos*

Words are the physicians of a mind diseased.

— **Aeschylus**, playwright (525-456 BCE), *Prometheus Bound*

ON THE COUCH

"My psychiatrist told me I'm going crazy. I told him, 'If you don't mind I'd like a second opinion.' He said, 'Alright... you're ugly too!'

– **Rodney Dangerfield**, comedian, actor (1921-2004), *comedy routine*

"But, you know, those three words – I need help. If only I'd said them earlier.

– **Elton John**, musician (1947-), *interview, Larry King Live, CNN*

"The thing that made me go for help, was probably my daughter. She was something that earthed me, grounded me, and I thought, this isn't right, this can't be right, she cannot grow up with me in this state.

– **J.K. Rowling**, author (1965-), *interview, Edinburgh University student magazine*

"Surely a good therapist should produce a Dorian Gray-style portrait from under the couch so the patient can see the person they really are.

– **Rosamund Lupton**, author (1964-), *Sister*

No further evidence is needed to show that 'mental illness' is not the name of a biological condition whose nature awaits to be elucidated, but is the name of a concept whose purpose is to obscure the obvious.

– **Thomas Szasz**, psychiatrist (1920-2012), *The Second Sin*

You take the cards you're dealt, and I got better. I'm now ferociously healthy in body and mind. You couldn't pay me to go near a psychiatrist again. Stopping seeing them was my first step to getting well.

– **Margot Kidder**, actor (1948-), *interview, Guardian*

"I proved to you that psychiatry is an exact science!"

"An exact science?!"

"Yes, you owe me exactly one hundred and forty-three dollars!"

– **Charles M. Schulz**, cartoonist, (1922-2000), *The Complete Peanuts*

Mental health ... is not a destination but a process. It's about how you drive, not where you're going. The therapist is like a driving instructor, not a chauffeur.

– **Noam Shpancer**, psychotherapist, author (1959-),
The Good Psychologist

Psychiatry's a young science. Yesterday's madman may be tomorrow's genius. Beethoven and Van Gogh were both a bit loopy. In my view, most madmen are remarkable. They're explorers, travellers beyond the rim of consciousness. Not surprising if they pick up a few bugs and get sick. That's all it is, madness. Mad just means sick. If you get fluid on the lungs it's pleurisy. If it's fluid on the brain, it's insanity.

– **Clare Boylan**, author, journalist (1948-2006),
Beloved Stranger

A psychiatrist is a man who goes to the Folies-Bergère and looks at the audience.

– **Mervyn Stockwood**, bishop (1913-1995), *Observer*

It's good to know that if I behave strangely enough, society will take full responsibility for me.

– **Ashleigh Brilliant**, author, cartoonist (1933-), *cartoon*

Some of the very greatest gifts bring an inevitable downside which you cannot "cure" without curing the gift at the same time.

– **Stephanie Tolan**, author (1942-),
interview, Gifted Women Forum

I decided early in graduate school that I needed to do something about my moods. It quickly came down to a choice between seeing a psychiatrist or buying a horse. Since almost everyone I knew was seeing a psychiatrist, and since I had an absolute belief that I should be able to handle my own problems, I naturally bought a horse.

– **Kay Redfield Jamison**, clinical psychologist (1946-),
An Unquiet Mind

What is the natural reaction when told you have a hopeless mental illness? "Well I might as well shoot myself now, because I'm going to disintegrate." And that diagnosis does you in; that, and the humiliation of being there. I mean, the indignity you're subjected to. My God.

– **Kate Millett**, author, activist (1934-), *interview, Consumer/Survivor/Ex-patient Oral History Project*

It's so weird that I went to rehab. I always said that I would die before I went to rehab. But I thought, 'I'm going to stay here tonight.' And I stayed there for a month. It was great.

– **Lindsay Lohan**, actor (1986-), *Allure magazine*

There is no psychology; there is only biography and autobiography.

– **Thomas Szasz**, psychiatrist (1920-2012), *The Second Sin*

I remember once I read a book on mental illness and there was a nurse that had gotten sick. Do you know what she died from? From worrying about the mental patients not being able to get their food. She became a mental patient.

– **Ornette Coleman**, musician (1930-), *Cadence magazine*

A neurotic is a man who builds a castle in the air. A psychotic is the man who lives in it. A psychiatrist is the man who collects the rent.

– **Robert Webb-Johnstone**, (1879-unknown), *Collected Papers*

Psychoanalysis is that mental illness for which it regards itself as therapy.

– **Karl Kraus**, journalist, playwright, poet (1874-1936), *Half-Truths and One-and-a-Half Truths*

The mystic sees the ineffable, and the psycho-pathologist the unspeakable.

– **W. Somerset Maugham**, writer, doctor (1874-1965), *The Moon and Sixpence*

If you talk to God, you are praying; If God talks to you, you have schizophrenia. If the dead talk to you, you are a spiritualist; If you talk to the dead, you are a schizophrenic.

– **Thomas Szasz**, psychiatrist (1920-2012), *The Second Sin*

It seems a pity that psychology has destroyed all our knowledge of human nature.

G. K. Chesterton, author (1874-1936), *London Observer*

If you cut a thing up, of course it will smell. Hence, nothing raises such an infernal stink, at last, as human psychology.

– **D. H. Lawrence**, author (1885-1930), *St. Mawr*

Men will always be mad, and those who think they can cure them are the maddest of all.

– **Voltaire**, philosopher (1694-1778), *letter*

There are now electrical appliances with the main unit so sealed in that it cannot be got at for repair. There have always been human beings like that.

– **Mignon McLaughlin**, writer (1913-1983),
The Complete Neurotic's Notebook

Our schizophrenic patient is actually experiencing inadvertently that same beatific ocean deep which the yogi and saint are ever striving to enjoy: except that, whereas they are swimming in it, he is drowning.

– **Joseph Campbell**, mythologist, writer (1904-1987), *Myths to Live By*

If you're really seriously, clinically depressed you care about nothing … Depression is the worst pain imaginable and it's almost inevitable that someone else has to get involved to get you out of it.

– **Phillip Hodson**, psychotherapist, broadcaster, author
(1946-), *BBC News website*

The physician should look upon the patient as a besieged city and try to rescue him with every means that art and science place at his command.

– **Alexander of Tralles**, physician (525-605CE),
Treatise on the Pathology and Therapeutics of Internal Diseases

I know each conversation with a psychiatrist in the morning made me want to hang myself because I knew I could not strangle him.

– **Antonin Artaud**, actor, producer
(1896-1948), *Van Gogh: The Man Suicided by Society*

Psychoanalysts are not occupied with the minds of their patients; they do not believe in the mind but in a cerebral intestine.

– **Bernard Berenson**, art critic (1865-1959), *quoted by Umberto Morra in Conversations with Berenson*

Healing is a matter of time, but it is sometimes a matter of opportunity.

– **Hippocrates**, physician (460-357 BCE), *Precepts*

It is not a case we are treating; it is a living, palpitating, alas, too often suffering fellow creature.

– **John Brown**, physician, author
(1810-1882), *Lancet*

Popular psychology is a mass of cant, of slush and of superstition worthy of the most flourishing days of the medicine man.

– **John Dewey**, philosopher (1859-1952),
The Public and its Problems

Psychology has a long past, but only a short history.

– **Hermann Ebbinghaus**, psychologist (1850-1909),
Summary of Psychology

Had there been a Lunatic Asylum in the suburbs of Jerusalem, Jesus Christ would infallibly have been shut up in it at the outset of his public career.

– **Havelock Ellis**, psychologist (1859-1939),
Impressions and Comments

The object of psychology is to give us a totally different idea of the things we know best.

— **Paul Valéry**, writer (1871-1945), *Tel Quel*

Nature has given man one tongue, but two ears, that we may hear twice as much as we speak.

— **Zeno of Elea,** philosopher (*c.* 490-430 BCE), *Fragments*

Talking about one's feelings defeats the purpose of having those feelings. Once you try to put the human experience into words, it becomes little more than a spectator sport. Everything must have a cause, and a name. Every random thought must have a root in something else.

— **Derek Landy**, author, screenwriter (1974-), *Death Bringer*

"I don't-" I shake my head. (...)

"What? What were you going to say?"

This is another trick of shrinks. They never let you stop in midthought. If you open your mouth, they want to know exactly what you had the intention of saying.

– **Ned Vizzini**, author (1981-2013), *It's Kind of a Funny Story*

I am interested in madness. I believe it is the biggest thing in the human race, and the most constant. How do you take away from a man his madness without also taking away his identity?

– **William Saroyan**, dramatist, author (1908-1981), *Short Drive, Sweet Chariot*

Freud: if it's not one thing, it's your mother.

– **Robin Williams**, actor and comedian (1951-2014), *comedy routine*

THE
STRAIGHT
DOPE

TAKE ONE A DAY AS DIRECTED

Half the modern drugs could well be thrown out the window, except that the birds might eat them.

– **Martin H. Fischer**, physician, author (1879-1962),
quoted in Fischerisms by Howard Fabing and Ray Marr

Despair is better treated with hope, not dope.

– **Richard Asher**, physician, writer
(1912-1969), *Lancet*

The mind like a sick body can be healed and changed by medicine.

– **Lucretius**, poet (*c.* 96-55BCE), *On the Nature of Things*

Patience is the best medicine.

– **John Florio**, linguist, lexicographer
(1553-1625), *First Fruits*

When you are dealing with a chemical imbalance in the brain, all the love in the world won't fix it.

– **Patty Duke**, actor (1946-), *Brilliant Madness*

"A miracle drug is any drug that will do what the label says it will do.

> – **Eric Hodgins**, writer, editor
> (1899-1971), *Episode*

Some drugs have been appropriately called 'wonder-drugs' inasmuch as one wonders what they will do next.

> – **Samuel Enoch Stumpf,** philosopher (1918-1998),
> *Tennessee Annals of Internal Medicine*

In my case, ECT was miraculous. My wife was dubious, but when she came into my room afterward, I sat up and said, 'Look who's back among the living.' It was like a magic wand.

> – **Dick Cavett**, chat show host (1936-),
> *interview, People magazine*

You just have to take a little salt [the drug sodium valproate], and since I'm doing that it's, like, BOOM! In one week, I felt it kick in. All the commotion around me, all the water around me, moving left and right around me, became like a lake.

– **Jean-Claude Van Damme**, martial artist, actor (1960-), *E! Online*

There are peaks, there are valleys. But they're all kind of carved and smoothed out, and it feels like a low level of despair you live in. Where you're not getting any answers, but you're living OK. And you can smile at the office. You know? But it's a low level of despair … I was on Prozac for a long time. It may have helped me out of a jam for a little bit, but people stay on it forever.

– **Jim Carrey**, actor (1962-), *interview, CBS*

And then, over and over, I would say I was sick – sick with any documented ailment I could think of except "depression," which no one, no matter what the brochures with grainy girls' pictures and the word "reuptake" say, will ever believe is a real sickness.

— **Virginia Heffernan**, journalist (1969-),
A Delicious Placebo

Looking back on it, I think this therapist was basically a groupie. He loved hearing stories of rock and roll and he started upping my dose. He watched me go from a beautiful, 125-pound, newly sober woman who had the world at her feet to a 170-pound woman who had the lights go out in her eyes.

— **Stevie Nicks**, singer-songwriter (1948-), *Newsweek*

TAKE HEART

Failure is an event, never a person.

> – **William D. Brown**, author, psychologist
> (1936-), *Welcome Stress!*

Every life deserves a certain amount of dignity, no matter how poor or damaged the shell that carries it.

> – **Rick Bragg**, author, journalist (1959-),
> *All Over but the Shoutin'*

What deep wounds ever closed without a scar?

> – **George Gordon Byron**, poet (1788-1824),
> *Child Harold's Pilgrimage*

Show me someone who has done something worthwhile, and I'll show you someone who has overcome adversity.

> – **Lou Holtz**, coach - American football (1937-),
> *quoted in Tales from the LSU Tigers Sideline*

Time is the great physician.

> – **Benjamin Disraeli,** prime minister, novelist
> (1804-81), *Henrietta Temple*

Sometimes even to live is an act
of courage.

— **Seneca**, philosopher (4 BCE-65CE), *letter*

You are unique, and if that is not fulfilled
then something has been lost.

— **Martha Graham**, dancer, choreographer
(1894-1991), *This I Believe, CBS*

Follow your inner moonlight;
don't hide the madness.

— **Allen Ginsberg**, poet (1926-1997),
interview, Writers Digest

Endure, and preserve yourselves for
better things.

— **Virgil**, poet (70-19 BCE), *The Aeneid*

Remember sadness is always temporary.
This, too, shall pass.

— **Chuck T. Falcon**, psychologist (1954-),
Overcoming Depression and Finding Happiness

"Madness need not be all breakdown. It may also be break-through. It is potential liberation and renewal as well as enslavement and existential death."

– **R. D. Laing**, psychiatrist (1927-1989),
The Politics of Experience

What happens is not as important as how you react to what happens.

– **Thaddeus Golas**, author (1924-1997),
The Lazy Man's Guide to Enlightenment

Nothing – not booze, not love, not sex, not work, not moving from state to state – will make the past disappear. Only time and patience heal things. I learned that cutting up your arms in an attempt to make the pain move from inside to outside, from soul to skin, is futile. That death is a cop-out. I tried all of these things.

– **Marya Hornbacher**, author, journalist
(1974-), *Voices From The Inside*

The feeling of being valuable - 'I am a valuable person'- is essential to mental health and is a cornerstone of self-discipline.

– **M. Scott Peck**, author, psychiatrist
(1936-2005), *The Road Less Travelled*

Our eternal message of hope is that dawn will come.

– **Martin Luther King, Jr.**, activist, clergyman
(1929-1968), *sermon, A Knock at Midnight*

How is it
People fear the dark?
Not me, I'm reconciled.
as every day I see
the blackness grow,
I've come to terms with it,
it knows I know.

– **Rod McKuen**, musician, poet (1933-), *Monochrome, Alone*

INDEX

MENTAL NOTES

Index

MENTAL NOTES

Index

About Bath Mind

Bath Mind is part of a network of local charities across the country, affiliated to the UK's leading mental health charity Mind. Local Minds support Mind's overall vision and mission and are responsible for providing services relevant to their local community:

Our vision
We won't give up until everyone experiencing a mental health problem gets both support and respect.

Our mission
We provide advice and support to empower anyone experiencing a mental health problem. We campaign to improve services, raise awareness and promote understanding.

Bath Mind reaches people in the Bath & North East Somerset area by providing information, short term housing, mentoring and advocacy, mental health training and support for community groups. These services are delivered by a small team of paid staff and a volunteer team who freely donate their skills, time and energy. The needs and experiences of people who live with a mental health problem drive our work and we ensure they are involved at every level of the organisation - as trustees, paid employees and volunteers.

mind | Bath
for better mental health

Mind has ambition for the future:
• Everyone will be aware of the importance of their own mental health.
• People will know where to turn for help if they become unwell.
• Help will be available whenever people need it, wherever they live.
• Recovery will be quicker and the impact of mental health
  problems reduced.
• Stigma and discrimination will be reduced significantly.

Bath Mind is committed to making that ambition a reality for the people of Bath & North East Somerset.

To find out how to support Bath Mind by giving a donation, becoming a member or joining the volunteer team go to www.bathmind.org.uk

Contact us at:
admin@bathmind.org.uk

About Kate McDonnell

Kate McDonnell has been Key Trustee for Community and Outreach at Bath Mind since early 2014.

Kate helped the Bath Mind-supported Mosaic group create their cookery book 'Mixed Spice', forwarded by chef Michael Caines MBE.

She also has two other books out – Beautiful Bath and Beastly Bath.

Kate also has a blog called the Bipolar Codex, which shows what it's like to be bipolar through drawings and the occasional quote. Her illustrations also feature in this book.

www.bipolarcodex.com

Acknowledgements

Kate McDonnell would like to thank Gideon Kibblewhite for editing, being generally wonderful and picking me up off the floor when necessary.

To Jackie Parrington for all her hard work and enthusiasm.

To Richard Jones of Tangent Books for all his help and support in getting this book published.

And to the team and members of Bath Mind, who are an inspiration, each and every day.

A medley of cultural cuisine

Mixed Spice brings together the favourite recipes from around the world of Bath's Mosaic social group. With the help of this book you can cook up a storm creating authentic warm, spicy delights from India, Asia, the Caribbean and other parts of the globe. Serve up and share flavoursome Finger Food, mouthwatering Meat, Fish and Vegetarian dishes and scrumptious Salads, Dips and Chutneys. Finish your feast with divine Cakes and Desserts.

Foreword by **Michael Caines MBE**:

"I am sure that each reader of Mixed Spice will find a recipe that will become their personal favourite."

Available now from **www.tangentbooks.co.uk** and **Bath Mind**

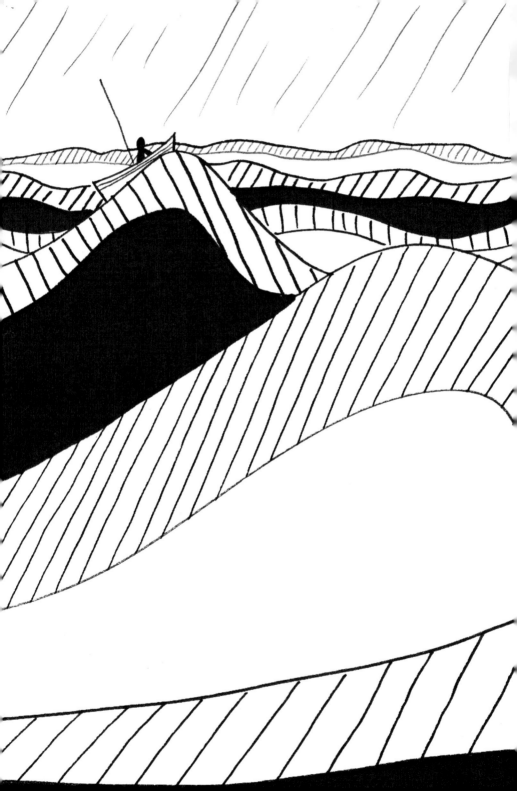